Memories of Antigua:
Books, Bugs, Bicycle Pumps, Beaches, and Blessings

Diane Findlay

Copyright © 2018 Diane Findlay

All rights reserved.

ISBN-13: 978-0-9862028-2-7

Cover Art Copyright © 2015 Deborah Eckert

Line Art Copyright © 2018 Marena Tunkin

DEDICATION

This book is dedicated to my family, who shared this adventure with me; to the lovely people of Antigua, especially Willikies, who patiently put up with us, educated us about their home and their lives, and allowed us to share what was precious to us; and to Bahá'í pioneers everywhere, past and present.

ACKNOWLEDGMENTS

Many thanks to Marena Tunkin and Deborah Eckert for their beautiful artwork, editor Cecelia Munzenmaier, and the readers who helped make this better—Bob, Naren, Linda, Jan, and Jean.

Memories of Antigua

CONTENTS

	Introduction	1
1	The Bushes Have Ears	2
2	So Pretty…	7
3	Antigua Mornings	10
4	Do Something!	14
5	Shameless Bribery	22
6	The Pied Piper of Willikies	26
7	Adjusting	30
8	Upside-Down Discrimination	40
9	"What's Wrong with Me?"	45
10	Free Therapy	49
11	On the Road	53
12	Contrast	59
13	"Squeeze the Eyes!"	67
14	It Seemed Like a Good Idea at the Time…	74
15	"We've Gotten Used to You"	82
16	Reflecting	86

INTRODUCTION

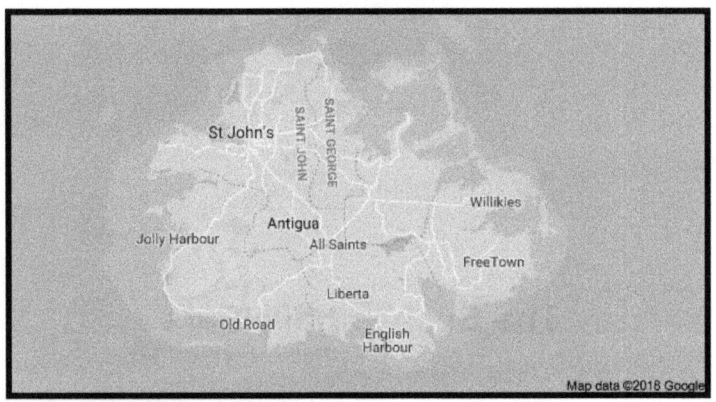

Antigua (officially Antigua and Barbuda) is located near the middle of the Leeward Island chain, with the Caribbean Sea on the west side and the Atlantic on the north and east. It's a parliamentary democracy that became an independent state within the British Commonwealth in 1981. It measures 54.1 miles around the coast with an area of 108 square miles. The capital city is St. John's. As of the 2011 census, the population just exceeded 80,000. The climate is tropical, prone to drought in the dry season and to hurricanes in the rainy season. And for a time, it was our home.

Diane Findlay

The Bushes Have Ears

It is natural for the heart and spirit to take pleasure and enjoyment in all things that show forth symmetry, harmony, and perfection. For instance: a beautiful house, a well designed garden..., a well written book... in fact, all things that have in themselves grace or beauty are pleasing to the heart and spirit.... ('Abdu'l-Bahá's words to Mrs. Mary L. Lucas, *A Brief Account of My Visit to Acca*, 1905, pp. 11-14)

It was May of 1982. Our family had just arrived in Antigua as Bahá'í pioneers—Bahá'ís who leave their homes to serve our faith, our fellow Bahá'ís, and their communities in other countries. We'd rented a house in Willikies, a little village on the east side of the Island, where we were the only white family. We'd spent the day unpacking. We knew we wanted to stay as long as we could, so we hadn't traveled light. And while we didn't know much yet about the Island's people and culture, we were fairly certain there wouldn't be a library every few miles, as we were used to at home. Being without ready access to books for us and our children, who were five and seven years old, was unthinkable. So we brought boxes of books. You have to know your priorities, right?

It was early evening and we were all tired, so I grabbed a handful of picture books and led the kids out to the gallery (what Americans call a porch) for our bedtime stories ritual. The house was littered with boxes and it was a lovely evening, so the gallery seemed the obvious choice. The kids planted themselves on the railings and I took the chair.

I started with the kids' favorite, *Alexander and the Terrible, Horrible, No Good, Very Bad Day* by Judith Viorst. I moved on to Gerald McDermott's *Arrow to the Sun*. They listened and enjoyed, but they were sleepily quiet. Partway into the second book, we heard a soft rustling in the hedge of hibiscus and gardenias that separated our house from the dirt road. There was a gentle breeze, so we didn't think much of it. But a few minutes later, we heard a muted giggle and I began to suspect. When the rustling began to sound like a scuffle, I was sure. The bushes had ears!

"Who's there?" I asked. "Please come out so we can meet you."

It took a little coaxing, but soon two small dark heads popped up above the hedge. We introduced ourselves and I asked if they were listening to the story. They nodded shyly, not meeting our eyes.

"Wouldn't you like to see the pictures? It's a picture book and the illustrations are wonderful. Come up on the gallery where you can see."

Memories of Antigua

They did. We read on. By the end of the third story, two teenage girls and a middle-aged man had appeared, also peeking over the hedge. I invited them to join us. Soon the gallery held us and half a dozen others, sharing the special joy of well-crafted picture books. We had made our first friends.

That was the first of many balmy, tropical evenings spent on the gallery, enjoying the fragrance of the gardenias and sharing stories. It was also the beginning of our discovering ways we could be of service in our new home. The village didn't have a library, literacy was growing but still spotty and, as I later learned, the pressures of slavery days had wiped out most of the oral storytelling tradition among these proud, life-loving people. They were hungry for good stories and we had them to spare! Some nights, when the gallery wasn't big enough for the dozen or so guests, we brought out extra chairs for the lawn so the grandmas and pregnant moms could listen in comfort.

To this day, one of my fondest memories is speaking out to the ears in the bushes and inviting the village in for stories.

So Pretty...

O God! O God! Thou seest my weakness, lowliness and humility before Thy creatures; nevertheless, I have trusted in Thee and have arisen in the promotion of Thy teachings among Thy strong servants, relying on Thy power and might. ('Abdu'l-Bahá, *Tablets of the Divine Plan*, 1977 Edition, p. 97)

On one of our first mornings in Willikies, we were unloading the last of the boxes from our little Toyota. Our daughter Naren, age five, and I were headed to the car for another load when something on the ground caught our eyes. Upon closer inspection, we discovered that it was a centipede, about five inches long, creamy white with a fuzzy pink stripe down its entire length. It was quite beautiful, for a bug. We "oohed and aahed" over it, bending down to get a closer look. As I reached out to touch it, we were startled by a frantic commotion. We looked up to see our neighbor, Matilda, running toward us in warrior mode, wielding a broom and shrieking like a banshee. We jumped back, bewildered and cowering. Matilda set upon the centipede with the broom, bashing as though her life depended on it!

We soon learned that, in a sense, it did. When the beautiful, colorful creature was reduced to a mushy stain on the gravel, Matilda looked at us like WE were the maniacs! She demanded to know, in her dense Island dialect, what we thought we were doing. We stammered timidly, something like, "It was so pretty...." Realizing that we pathetic Americans really were that ignorant, she patiently explained that the "pretty" bug was deadly, with a bite that could kill or at least make you very sick.

Memories of Antigua

That moment was one of many over the early days and weeks of our stay that wore away any illusions we had about being in a position, due to our American education and economic advantages, to "help" and "teach" the people around us. We shifted into humble, receptive mode and began to learn.

But it really was pretty…

Antigua Mornings

O God, my God! Thou seest me... enkindled with the fire of Thy love amongst mankind... entreating and invoking Thee at morn and at eventide to graciously aid me to serve Thy Cause, to spread abroad Thy Teachings and to exalt Thy Word throughout the East and the West. ('Abdu'l-Bahá, *Tablets of the Divine Plan*, 1977 Edition, pp. 43-44)

I am not a morning person—never have been. But mornings in Antigua were something special. During our first week in the Willikies house we were awakened VERY early one morning by an alarming noise. It was somewhere between a foghorn and an asthmatic wheeze, and it repeated itself with painful persistence. My husband Bob and I jumped up and ran to the window, unsure whether someone was dying right outside or the village was under attack. What did we see? A sway-backed, flea-bitten donkey, tethered in the empty lot next to our yard, who apparently considered it his job to be sure no one overslept. Have you ever heard a donkey in full-throated, insistent bray? It's like no other sound on earth, and definitely not what I wanted to hear at 5:00 AM! Someone had obviously left him in the lot to forage for whatever meager growing things he could find on that scrabbly patch of ground.

Once our panic subsided and our pulses slowed, we realized that our vocal equine friend was not the only one up so early. We began to sense other evidence of the village stirring to life. We heard neighbors, mostly women, shuffling along the road. We watched from the window. They ambled toward the water catchment, carrying large containers on their heads, to fetch water for the day. Our first response was to pity these poor people, whose lives were bereft of even the most basic conveniences we took for granted. But that feeling quickly gave way to amazement, as we realized the women were singing or whistling as they made their way along the road. Their cheerful tunes and warm greetings to each other dispelled our pity. We realized that, while the villagers were certainly poor by our American standards, they were neither pitiable nor unhappy. They found joy in their lives, even at 5:00 in the morning, even burdened with the load they carried. Again came the humbling experience of glimpsing how much we had to learn from our new friends and neighbors.

The donkey wasn't often left outside our window, and we did eventually develop some grudging affection for the sad-looking critter. We got used to the sounds of Willikies and its residents waking and starting the day, too early for our liking. The songs, whistled tunes, warm greetings—even the sickly braying—became familiar, welcome background to our gradual emergence from sleep. And, once in a while, I even got up willingly to appreciate the dawn.

Memories of Antigua

For me, the best reason to get out of bed before light was to jump in the car and drive across the Island to Shirley Heights. Now and then, on a holy day or other special occasion, we would meet fellow Bahá'ís at that gorgeous spot, overlooking English Harbor, for dawn prayers. Perhaps it was some magic of the light or the departure from routine. Maybe it was the elevation, suggestive of distancing ourselves from everyday life and making a closer approach to the mysteries "above." But I've rarely experienced morning prayers as potent or glorious as they were on those days.

I'm still not a morning person—probably never will be. And I promise you, a donkey's bray will never be my choice of sound for a programmable alarm clock! But I remember mornings in Antigua with a sweet fondness that transcends my personal rhythms and makes me smile every time.

Do Something!

...Plans are concrete things, and not mere honors, and victories—like all other achievements in life—must be purchased at the cost of persistent efforts! (Shoghi Effendi, *Messages to Canada*, 1965 edition, p. 145)

We arrived in Antigua full of zeal to charge in and be of service. As Bahá'í pioneers we knew that we would, in some fashion, be sharing our teachings, helping local Bahá'ís develop their distinctive communities, and serving the wider community in which we lived. We couldn't wait to get started!

Memories of Antigua

A couple of weeks after our arrival, we headed to Falmouth to meet with the National Spiritual Assembly of the Bahá'ís of the Leeward Islands. Bob and I had both served on Local Spiritual Assemblies, the administrative institutions that guide the development of local Bahá'í communities, in Iowa and Utah, but we'd never had the opportunity to meet with a National Assembly before. We were thrilled! It was a privilege to meet the individuals elected to serve, and to consult with them as a body. Even the kids, at some level, appreciated this rare opportunity and insisted on coming along. We arrived full of gratitude and eager to have the Assembly explain our roles and give us our marching orders.

The nine members of the Assembly welcomed us with such warmth and love! They had expanded their circle of chairs in the living room of the unofficial matriarch of the Antigua Bahá'í community, Doris Francis, and her husband, to make room for all four of us. We felt honored, humbled, and a little nervous. But the joyful, shining faces around us, ranging from palest white to darkest brown, banished our shyness. We prayed together. They took turns describing, frankly and lovingly, the condition and activities of the Bahá'í communities on the Island, and asked about our skills and interests. Doris served tea and sweets and the conversation became more casual. It was obvious our time with them was coming to a close. This was it! Now they would tell us what they wanted us to do. But the assignments we'd awaited didn't come. The Assembly members were rising from their chairs to usher us out, with heartfelt encouragements to "get out there and DO SOMETHING!"

What? "Do something?" Do WHAT? We were stunned! As we drove back to Willikies, the kids chattered about the people we'd met and the tasty treats. Bob and I rode in silence. What were we supposed to do now? We both felt a touch of panic. We'd made this enormous decision, given up good jobs, packed up our lives, and come to this unfamiliar place on a leap of faith, and now we had no idea what we were doing here!

Over the next few days we thought a lot, talked a lot, prayed a lot. We reviewed the meeting and its surprising conclusion. And we realized that we were not totally without guidance, after all. The Assembly members had described what other pioneers were doing, in response to needs in their particular communities. They had encouraged us to meet the Willikies Bahá'ís, to get to know the village and its people, to watch and to listen. Slowly, gradually, we began to understand. Our role was to observe, learn, assess, and find creative ways to address needs among the Bahá'ís and the general population, as we saw them. We were not to approach our task with predetermined expectations or to carry out externally-contrived plans. We were to make friends, build community connections, listen, pray, and serve as conditions suggested. So we began to get to know the Bahá'ís, their families, and their circumstances.

We also weren't on our own. We met the other pioneers on the Island, mostly from the USA or Canada. We teamed up with another pioneer family and were assigned several villages to learn about and focus on. The Baloghs, from Canada, weren't quite as green as we were, having arrived several months earlier. We enjoyed them. We clicked. And we benefited from their experience and already-formed friendships and insights. Their children and ours made friends and, together, made friends with Antiguan kids around us.

As we ventured out to our assigned villages, we quickly learned that there were few, if any, street signs. Directions went something like this: "Oh, you looking for Boku? Follow this way and turn right at the cashew tree. He be right there." Being Americans, we asked if there were maps. "No maps, mon. See the cashew tree." So, for our own use, we began to sketch maps of the villages, filling in landmarks (yes, some were cashew trees) and marking the houses of Bahá'ís and other new friends. The villagers saw us consulting these papers and wanted to know what they were. Amazing!—They were absolutely gleeful to see maps, even as rudimentary as ours, that showed their houses, their bakeries, their water catchments, right there in black and white. Apparently, no one had ever considered their villages important enough to map before, at least in that much detail. They wanted copies. So Bob and Len Balogh set about creating accurate, roughly-to-scale maps of our villages, by hand, to distribute and post in shops. They were a hit!

As we visited the Bahá'ís in our villages, they often asked about Bahá'ís in other parts of the Island. What with long working hours, inefficient transportation, and no telephones (except at the local police stations), they had trouble staying in touch with personal friends and had no knowledge of scheduled Bahá'í activities. Aha! As a lifelong "word nerd," that was my cue—a lightbulb switched on! *The Leeward Link*, a monthly newsletter for the Bahá'ís of the several Leeward Islands that made up our "national" administrative community, was born. It included features on individual Bahá'ís, schedules of events, and news about plans, gatherings, and accomplishments, as well as prayers, selections from Bahá'í scriptures, simple study guides, and devotional pieces. It started out heavy on Antiguan news, as ours was the biggest

Island and home base of the National Spiritual Assembly. But, gradually, the other Islands began to send us news and the National Assembly fed us details about events, past and future. I composed the newsletter on an old manual typewriter and took it to a copy shop in St. John's for printing. We mailed copies to the other Islands, passed copies to other pioneer teams for their villages, and delivered them around our villages in person. It gave us a focus for our visits. Surprisingly, our little newsletter soon became a literacy tool, as the children in the families we visited read them with and to their semi-literate mothers and illiterate grandmothers. We were always welcomed when we visited the friends in our villages, but we were especially welcome if we had "the newspaper" to share. Conversation took off: "Where does it say that?" "Is my name in there?"

My trips to St. John's to shop or copy the newsletter usually included a stop at the Island's little public library, and before long I was volunteering there weekly. Our evening story times evolved to include an informal lending library and we gradually ventured into loaning out the tools Bob had brought, as our neighbors needed them.

And before we knew it—what do you know?—we were quite busy, "doing something."

Shameless Bribery

This great bounty will dawn over the world at the time when the lovers of God shall arise to carry out His Teachings, and to scatter far and wide the fresh, sweet scents of universal love. ('Abdu'l-Bahá, *Selections from the Writings of 'Abdu'l-Bahá*, 1978, p. 20)

As we settled into life in Antigua, we were eager to share the message and teachings of our Faith with the people around us. Along with casual conversations with neighbors and friends, Bahá'ís often approach this through meetings in our homes, called "firesides," at which we offer hospitality and information on various aspects of Bahá'í beliefs. These gatherings might involve prayers, music, speakers, videos, art, games, drama, or other modes of sharing and interacting. We wanted to start hosting firesides and had plenty of new friends to invite. But there were complications.

Many of our new friends worked hard all day (after getting up early, as I've mentioned), and came home to the chore of preparing dinner for their families. This was not a quick and easy task when the primary cooking method was a pot over a coal burner. They had children to tend and laundry and other everyday chores to complete, and they were tired.

We quickly learned that if we were even going to try evening gatherings, we had to choose our evening carefully. While few of the villagers had electricity in their homes, it seemed they all had battery-powered television sets and were collectively addicted to Worldwide Wrestling Entertainment on Monday nights! Nothing—and I mean nothing—else was planned on Monday evenings.

We settled on Wednesdays, made our plans, and issued invitations. The first couple of Wednesdays several friends arrived, only a few minutes after the designated time. Considering the Islanders' relaxed attitude toward time, that was gratifying in itself. According to custom, they called out, "Inside!" from the road (the Antiguan equivalent of knocking on the door) and entered the house, shyly at first. We served tea and gave our little presentations. It took some coaxing to get our guests involved in discussion, but gradually, they participated with increasing comfort and interest. Still, only a few attended and conversation was somewhat strained.

The first time we served cake, we had no idea the stunning effect it would have on the event. Our small group of guests pointed and giggled. They consumed every last crumb in record time and, perhaps fueled by the extra sugar, jumped into lively discussion. It was an exhilarating evening! The next week, we offered fresh, local fruits. Our guests were polite, but asked, "Will there be cake?" It finally dawned on us (slow learners that we were) that our house was one of only a few in the village that had an actual indoor oven. Baked goods like cakes and pies were rare treats.

Armed with this knowledge, we consulted and agreed that we were not at all above shameless bribery! Cake mixes were cheap (unlike the honey we had to ration, as our sweet-toothed neighbors set upon it like parched desert wanderers at an oasis). We began to offer cake every week, and our meetings took off. Attendance grew rapidly as word spread and, with it, our opportunities to spread the word about our Faith. One final adjustment—serving tea and cake at the beginning of the evening, rather than later, to ensure that guests arrived in time for the program—and we were on our way. We and our guests discussed challenging questions, shared wide-ranging perspectives, and enjoyed a spirited and spiritually satisfying level of discourse. And all it took was respecting the sacredness of Monday night wrestling and cake!

The Pied Piper of Willikies

The education and training of children is among the most meritorious acts of humankind and draweth down the grace and favour of the All-Merciful, for education is the indispensable foundation of all human excellence and alloweth man to work his way to the heights of abiding glory. ('Abdu'l-Bahá, *Selections from the Writings of 'Abdu'l-Bahá*, 1978, p. 129)

A few weeks into our stay, Linda, another American Bahá'í pioneer who had spent many years on the Island, invited us to join her for a children's class in our village. How exciting! We were sure our kids would enjoy it, and we'd taught children's classes in our home communities and at regional Bahá'í summer schools in Iowa and Utah, so this was familiar territory—or so we thought. But the morning of our first class, we realized that we'd never seen anything quite like this before.

Linda parked her car in our driveway and pulled out her guitar. She motioned for us to follow and set off down the road, strumming as she went. We spent the next twenty minutes or so following her along the village roads and pathways as she sang enthusiastically, "Bahá'u'lláh has come and the watchword now is UNITY…" to the tune of "Bingo." As we strolled she attracted children to our growing parade, in full-out Pied Piper mode.

What seemed quaint and adventurous to us was, apparently, familiar to the children, who fell in line full of smiles and giggles, skipping and playfully shoving, some singing along. By the time Linda had wound her way through the village and come to a stop under a large, welcoming tree that offered a spacious, shaded "classroom" under its branches, there were fifteen or twenty children ready to sit on blankets spread on the ground and take in whatever came next. We were charmed! It was so spontaneous and natural, so different from the carefully planned, fun-but-oh-so-orderly classes we were used to. We sat with the children, delighted by the casual flow of prayers, songs, games, coloring, and stories that followed.

An hour flew by, filled with joy and spirit and occasional tussles, gently defused with a simple word or raised eyebrow. There were even sweet, short quotations from the Bahá'í Writings, recited from memory by children who had learned them during previous classes. We were amazed at how eagerly these children, who didn't have all the latest toys and distractions our kids were used to at home, embraced the simple lesson plan and how eagerly they participated in whatever Linda offered them. It all felt beautifully free of weighty expectations and richly "in the moment." We reveled in the simple sharing of God's love, of fun and happiness and, yes, unity.

Later classes followed this pattern, with smaller or larger groups of children, more or less peace or chaos, sometimes involving false starts or challenges, especially when we who were new to this mode took the lead. But it was always joyful, nourishing, and fun.

I still teach Bahá'í children's classes. I carefully plan and try to maintain some semblance of order, and I struggle, sometimes, with expectations. I don't always succeed in embracing the level of spontaneous, unscripted joy I felt in Willikies. But I love the experience and the opportunity and, most of all, the children, with a simple pleasure that grows from and calls upon the fresh tropical breezes and uncomplicated, radiant example of those purely satisfying mornings.

Adjusting

The believers must rest assured that, having the Faith, they have everything. They must place their lives in the Hand of God, and, confident of His mercy and protection, go on teaching the Cause and serving it, no matter what happens. (Shoghi Effendi, *Dawn of a New Day*, May 8, 1942, p. 191)

It's a tricky thing, accustoming yourself to life in a new country. I'd read that culture shock is, largely, a matter of mental fatigue, from having to be constantly alert and think about every tiny decision in a day, without the many cultural cues and props we take for granted at home. While our experience of culture shock was not extreme, it was significant and real. So many things to learn, to process, to adjust to; so many assumptions to discard and values to rethink.

There were physical adjustments, of course, that happened quite naturally. The time difference was not difficult, being only five hours later than Utah, where we moved from. Arriving in August, as we did, the climate adjustment wasn't extreme, though the effects of humidity during the rainy season—never feeling completely dry—took some getting used to. Within a short time, we were so acclimated that "winter" temperatures, in the 70s, sent us looking for sweaters!

The real challenges were subtler. While shifting time zones was relatively simple, accepting the cultural attitude toward time was not. We were Americans, and Americans raised to prize punctuality, at that. My father had always believed that if you weren't ten minutes early, you were late, and that was simply unacceptable. But Antigua, while not part of Latin America, is very much a "mañana culture," when it comes to time. What does that mean? *Mañana,* of course, means "tomorrow" in Spanish. But in cultural context, it also means "some unspecified time in the future." It doesn't so much imply "twenty-four hours from now" as it does "not now, maybe later." A good example is the regional airline, LIAT (Leeward Islands Air Transport), more commonly and resignedly known as "Leave Island Any Time."

My personal theory is that the warmer and more tropical the climate, the slower people move and the less clock-oriented they become. Even Bahá'ís who were visiting from more time-conscious cultures seemed to slow to a crawl when they reached the Islands. At any rate, we had some major mental reorientation to accomplish. Not that our promptness was always a bad thing—locals and more seasoned pioneers soon learned that the best way to deal with us was simply to give us the key to whatever meeting space we were using, knowing that we'd have the site open, set up, and ready whenever the rest arrived. They'd chuckle, thank us, and move on.

The problem was more one of attitude. We had to learn not to be annoyed when friends we'd arranged to visit at 3:00 weren't home when we got there. They'd usually saunter in within forty-five minutes or so, happy to see us but completely oblivious of the clock. We had to learn not to schedule more than a couple of things in a day, since we never knew precisely when events would begin or end.

This flexible approach to time seemed to extend to the weather, as well. The rainy season featured frequent, awe-inspiringly torrential downpours, which pretty much stopped everyone in their tracks. Even we understood that there was little choice but to take shelter and wait it out. But lighter showers didn't deter us. We assumed life would go on as usual. One morning we set out to one of our villages to visit and deliver *The Leeward Link* to Bahá'í families. They had our schedule down and would be expecting us and eager to see the latest issue. The rain was moderate and made driving and walking through the village wet, muddy propositions, but we soldiered on and reached the first house. Dripping and soggy, we stood on the road and hollered, "Inside! Inside!" No response. Eventually, our Bahá'í friend cracked open the door and peered out, eyes widening in wonder. Her greeting—"You came? In the rain?"

The scarcity of simple comforts we took for granted was another challenge. We wanted to live in the village, experiencing life as much like the locals did as possible. But we needed a car. And foregoing things like running water, electricity, and basic cooking appliances was more than we could manage. So we compromised. We bought a cheap little Toyota. We found a house to rent that had cold (not hot) running water, electricity, and a kitchen with a stove and oven. The water usually did warm up to tolerable shower temperature by late afternoon. We even bought a primitive washing machine, which found its home in the carport.

And that prompted another adjustment. We were living on savings while we looked for work, so we tried to be as frugal as possible. Yet we were absolutely expected, as "rich" white expatriates, to employ a local woman to do laundry for us. So we did. Our neighbor, Matilda, came over regularly to use our washing machine (a luxury, in her eyes) and hang our laundry on the lines in the yard.

Language was another interesting adjustment. As we'd approached the move, everyone we talked to and everything we read assured us that Antiguans spoke English. Whew! Sadly, like too many Americans, we were not competent in any other language. However, the reality on Island was quite different. Yes, Antiguans spoke English. But everyday life is conducted in a thick dialect that incorporates Africanisms and Creole influences with Standard English. Some said it was deliberately developed, during Colonial days, to allow field laborers to talk freely without the British overseer understanding the conversation. It is rich and lilting and lovely to the ear, but we found it largely incomprehensible.

Sometimes, out of consideration for us, our neighbors would switch into the proper, British

English they had learned in school and could summon at will. But much of the time, we were simply baffled. Kids being kids, our children caught on to the local parlance quickly, and took full advantage of the opportunity to carry on their own conversations, leaving us none the wiser. Who knows what devious plots they concocted and carried out during that phase? They're not telling!

Eventually our ears attuned and we were able to understand most, if not all, of what was going on around us. We never learned to speak it. We didn't have to. Everyone understood us just fine and it felt presumptuous, somehow, to try to imitate the local accent and expressions. But, to this day, in private conversations, we're likely to substitute "You tief me pen?" for "Did you take my pen?" or "t'all, t'all" for "not at all," or "likkle" for "little," or to blame bad luck on the "jumbies." *

Beyond language, communication around the Island and beyond it was limited by the general absence of telephones. In the villages, people used the phone at the local police station when they needed to reach someone farther away. That's why our phone calls to family or friends in the States were few and far between. On-Island plans for activities or visits relied on the local mail service or word of mouth. Our Bahá'í newsletter filled a real need for believers hungry for news within and between the Leeward Islands Bahá'í communities, but it had to be delivered by post or by hand. Mostly, we remembered to arrange the next meeting or visit before leaving the last one, and hope for the best. Things are different now, with cell phones and the Internet. That's good! But I have to laugh, as I imagine people with today's addiction to instant communication, time-traveling back just thirty-five years to Antigua in the 1980s. Talk about culture shock! They would wonder how we survived at all.

Food was quite different. While housing was relatively inexpensive, food was not. Of course, the tropical climate supported wonderful local produce like mangoes, papayas, plantains, pineapples, and coconuts. But many food products were imported and, therefore, quite pricey. Farming was painfully associated with slave labor, and few Antiguans wanted to do it. They even imported fish! We could get many foods we were used to at a small import shop that catered to expatriates, but living on a budget required careful choices. We came to love the local fruits and learned to make some local dishes, but I'd be lying if I didn't admit we yearned for a Big Mac now and then.

All that adjusting can test a person's patience and confidence. Sometimes we felt discouraged and inadequate. But we knew we were learning and growing, and hoped we were serving and helping. Through it all, the great and unexpected blessing was a growing sense of relying on God, in ways and to extents we'd never experienced before. By about Christmas time, 1982, we'd bumbled our way through most of our culture shock. We were ready to enjoy a holiday season decked out in vibrant red hibiscus, and to delight in familiar Christmas carols played heartily and exotically (to our ears) on steel drums. Winter doldrums and the drab grays of lingering snow seemed far away. We were home.

Memories of Antigua

*Jumbies are evil or mischievous spirits in the folklore of Antigua and other English-speaking Caribbean countries.

Upside-Down Discrimination

The diversity in the human family should be the cause of love and harmony, as it is in music where many different notes blend together in the making of a perfect chord. ('Abdu'l-Bahá, quoted in *Advent of Divine Justice*, 1938, p.32)

Standard dictionaries define "discrimination" something like this: "The state of treating a person or group of people differently than others due to an observable or definable difference, usually in ways that disrespect or disadvantage them."

Moving to Antigua from the USA, with its ugly,

subversive, and complex history of race relations, we had no idea what our experience would be. We knew we would be part of a small minority of white-skinned, Anglo-background people on the Island, at least as residents—white tourists were plentiful. How would we be received? Would we face discrimination? Would we find distressing traces of racism in ourselves? A couple of people with experience on the Island warned us to guard our possessions and never loan anything, based on the assumption that the locals would see us as white and therefore, by definition, rich, and feel free to steal from us.

We were, I admit, guarded at first. We were certainly an oddity in the village. But we moved into a house in the middle of Willikies, put our children in the local school, and invited neighbors into our home. Those actions began to whittle away at potential assumptions and barriers. The first loans were books, sent home with eager children after evening stories on the gallery. Early on, children saw Bob using a bicycle pump and patch kit to fix the tires on the kids' rickety bikes, and asked to borrow the pump. It became a popular circulating item from the Findlay "library," along with various other tools.

At first, we loaned only to kids we knew well in the neighborhood. But we gave up trying to screen and keep track once we discovered that an item borrowed from us often made its way through several pairs of hands before coming back to us. Bob developed a strategy. He'd tell one of the kids in the neighborhood that he needed his—whatever it was—the next day. And sure enough, it worked! The item in question would be waiting on the carport steps when he checked the next morning. I don't believe we lost a single item from this rather random circulating collection. The more we interacted with the people around us in ordinary, everyday ways as neighbors and friends, the more comfortable and trusting those relationships became, and the word spread. We were still an oddity, but a generally well-accepted oddity.

The children were another story, entirely. They quickly became favorites in the village—almost mascots. Their white-blond hair and very light skin (though darkening in the intense Antiguan sun), along with their friendly, outgoing, and curious natures, seemed to endear them to the neighbors, who spoiled them. Their new friends gave them village nicknames and taught them how to suck the gummy syrup out of sugar cane stalks. Older neighbors treated them to the choicest fresh fruits. They learned and passed on to us "the right way to eat a mango." * What they experienced was a sort of "upside-down discrimination," which worked almost entirely to their advantage.

Here's an example. The commerce around fruit on the Island was interesting, at least in the villages. By general consensus, each mango or coconut tree, each finger banana, plantain, or pineapple plant belonged to some specific person, whether or not it was on their property. They used the fruits themselves and then sold the surplus by simply setting themselves up in visible spots around the village until their stock was gone. Coming home from errands in St. John's one day, we noticed a woman sitting on an overturned bucket at a street corner, with a huge bag of mangoes to sell. When we got home, we gave Nathan a few EC (Eastern Caribbean) dollars—the currency used on the Island—and sent him back to buy some mangoes for the family. He returned after about ten minutes, dragging the whole bag of mangoes behind him! That settled it. We knew who would be doing our local shopping from that day on!

* There are few things juicier or more stain-producing than ripe Antiguan mangoes. Here's "the right way" to eat one: First, unless you don't care about your clothes, put on your special mango-eating shirt. Second, squeeze the fruit gently with your hands to soften it up and loosen the flesh from the skin. Third, bite off the top. Finally, suck out the luscious contents and revel in the sticky sweetness!

"What's Wrong with Me?"

Humanity may be likened unto the vari-colored flowers of one garden. There is unity in diversity. Each sets off and enhances the other's beauty.
('Abdu'l-Bahá, *Divine Philosophy*, 1918, pp. 25-26)

As soon as we got settled, we enrolled our children in the village school. The level of education was not what we were used to, but we knew we could supplement with a correspondence curriculum and felt they would gain much of value by experiencing the local school. We, and they, were warmly welcomed by the staff. The principal was so receptive that he offered us use of the school building for Bahá'í activities. We got the information we needed, had their orange gingham uniform clothing made (shirts for Nathan, dresses for Naren), and sent them off to begin the school year.

They both made friends easily and chattered enthusiastically about their first days in class. Their teachers reported good adjustments. We settled into a comfortable routine of school days, followed by supplemental coursework at home. We were pleased.

You can imagine my surprise then, when Naren came home for lunch one afternoon sobbing uncontrollably. While we sometimes teasingly called her "Sarah Bernhardt" because of her emotional expressiveness, she was not really given to excessive drama. So I was baffled and a little alarmed. It took several minutes to calm her enough to catch her breath. When she could manage, she let out a wail. "What's wrong with me?"

How was I supposed to answer that? Had she hurt

herself? Had someone bullied her? Eventually, she regained enough composure to explain. Just before morning dismissal, the girls in her class had been sitting outside, plaiting each other's hair. But when it was Naren's turn, the plaits wouldn't hold—they fell right out of her straight, fine, blond hair. No matter how hard the girls tried or what techniques they used, they simply could not get her hair to hold the plaits securely, as theirs did. Apparently, they'd been kind but didn't know what to do. Obviously (in Naren's mind), something was very wrong!

Once I understood, I was overcome with relief. Such a simple thing to get so worked up about! I had to stifle a chuckle; what she needed from me was sympathy and reassurance. She was distraught and identifying so completely with her cultural surroundings that she saw her differentness as failure, even if no one else did. It didn't take long to demonstrate, with a little help from a neighbor girl, the differences in texture between our hair (mine as much as hers) and that of most of the girls and women around us, and to convince her that the differences were fine and natural, and far from being a handicap or flaw, were a lovely way that God made us interesting. I found some rubber bands, which allowed her to sport a silky braid or two of her own. By the time she went back to school, she was her happy, confident self.

We've laughed many times over the years, remembering this small, but powerful, crisis. To this day, I feel for her and marvel at how innocently her open heart accepted all we had thrown at her, and how easy it can be to experience difference as inadequacy.

Free Therapy

Prescribe for them then through Thy Pen of Glory that which will direct their steps to the ocean of Thy generosity and will lead them unto the living waters of Thy heavenly reunion. (Bahá'u'lláh, *Tablets of Bahá'u'lláh*, 1978, p. 177)

Antigua prides itself on having 365 beaches—one for each day of the year. I can't say that I've counted them, and some are tiny and secluded, but I'm inclined to credit the claim. All the Island's beaches are open to the public, so you just have to try some and choose your favorites.

The closest beach to us in Willikies was Long Bay, about a mile east along a rutted dirt road. Very early on, we came to think of this lovely nearby spot as our source of free personal therapy. Despite being on the less-protected Atlantic side of the Island, its waves were usually gentle and the sand was fine, light brown sugar, warm and caressing beneath our feet. Birds twittered soothingly, tiny sand crabs popped up and scuttled along playfully, and the vastness of the ocean beyond offered peace and perspective. Sometimes, if we were lucky, a steel drum band would be rehearsing within earshot. We went often—several times each week. And while we acclimated quickly to the warm climate, winter's cooler water temperatures were never enough to discourage us. We walked, waded, splashed, swam, snorkeled, or sunbathed at the prompting of our moods.

Sometimes we walked to and from, as most of our neighbors did. But as we got busier, we started driving to save a little time. Our car was small, but that never prevented the neighbor kids from asking to ride along. Rides to the beach were luxurious novelties, much sought after. We were happy to oblige and often managed to fit three or four extras into (or half out of) our little Toyota. Some evenings we'd come outside after supper, with a trip to the beach in mind, to find half a dozen hopefuls loitering along the road, eager to jump aboard. Competition became fierce enough that we had to devise a system to keep track of who rode when and whose turn was next.

We had other favorite beaches. It's hard to live on Antigua and not become a bit of a beach connoisseur. Half Moon Bay had lovely rolling waves just right for playing in or body surfing. Reaching Rendezvous Bay required a longish hike on a rough trail between hills, but was very much worth the trouble! It was never crowded—in fact, we were sometimes the only people there. Conjure up your most tantalizing tropical beach fantasy— gently waving palm trees, white sugar sand, fresh coconuts to be had for the picking, the soft swooshing of incoming waves, lush scents of salt air and fragrant flowers... That's Rendezvous Bay.

It's where Nathan learned to shinny up the coconut palms to knock down snacks for the family. It's perhaps the best picnic spot on the planet, if you don't mind lugging your provisions over the trail.

Eventually, we started heading across the Island to Jolly Beach on Sunday mornings for volleyball and swimming at one of the many resorts, with a group of friends and acquaintances, old and new. The size and make-up of the group varied week to week, but the games were always vigorous and the conversation lively. Sometimes, they became deep discussions of spiritual matters and Bahá'í teachings. But if not, we were content to play and socialize.

No, we didn't sample all 365 beaches. And no, we didn't turn into lazy beach bums. But no matter how tired or stressed or out-of-place we felt, Antigua's beaches invited us to rest, play, warm our skin, cleanse our minds with meditation, and soothe our spirits. You simply can't buy that kind of therapy!

On the Road

Look thou around the world of existence: A little worldly transaction cannot be brought about except through surmounting many an obstacle. How much more important are the objects of the Supreme World! Certainly there existeth troubles, trials, afflictions… But the end of all these is bliss, overflowing joy, everlasting exultation, happiness and supreme contentment…. ('Abdu'l-Bahá, *Tablets of 'Abdu'l-Bahá Volume 3*, 1980, p. 548)

I've described driving to the nearby beach with three or four extra passengers hanging out of our little car. This habit of ignoring maximum capacity recommendations for vehicles was commonplace, extending to the buses that carried villagers to and from work, which often had locals waving from the windows and spilling out of open doors at high-traffic times. And that practice was just one of many things that made driving Antigua's roads an unending adventure.

Let's start with directional signs or, more accurately, the lack thereof! Most major roads were identified here and there along the way. Signs led to tourist attractions, like resorts, Shirley Heights, Nelson's Dockyard, or the island's one small remaining rain forest. Most smaller roads were not marked, so finding our way was often a matter of landmarks and luck. Anything could be a landmark, for purposes of verbal directions—a grove of trees, a bright yellow village store, a small church that looked pretty much like every other small church in the area, or even "the corner where Mrs. Henry sells baskets." There were few accurate maps and even those were hard to follow, with little in the way of road signage to match to the winding routes marked on paper. The situation improved as you approached St. John's, but finding your way to town was by guess and by gosh. Of course, over time we became familiar with the routes to the villages our teaching team visited and to the friends and businesses we frequented. But for someone like me, born without the gene for directional sense, it was a constant challenge.

Once we committed to a route, there were other hazards to keep us on our toes. At any moment, a flock of goats or chickens or a donkey might trot out and meander across or down the road ahead of us, confident in their right of way and oblivious to vehicles around them. They seemed never to be in a hurry and shouts or car horns had no effect whatsoever.

If we weren't dodging livestock, we were careening back and forth to avoid bumps and dips in the pavement. Road maintenance was not a high priority, and some potholes were large enough to swallow one of the above-mentioned goats! We learned which roads were worst but didn't always have alternate choices. The common response of local drivers to these challenges was to brake suddenly when approaching a known hazard and then speed up once past it to make up for lost time. This made for interesting road-sharing experiences. Let's just say you could never let your guard down or count on your car's suspension system to last more than a year.

Then there were the "cassie" thorns. Cassie bushes were everywhere and their thorns were a menace. They could grow to an inch or more in length and seemed to have the tensile strength of steel spikes! They lurked on roadways, with the evil intent of puncturing your tires and, unlike large potholes, you had little hope of seeing and dodging them. Flat tires were "business as usual" and these wicked little weapons accounted for much of the popularity of our often-borrowed bicycle pump.

I remember one Thursday when I was making my way to St. John's for my weekly volunteer shift at the public library. I was to present a children's storytime program at 10:00 AM. Suddenly my car seemed to develop a mind of its own! It veered sharply right and came to a stop just off the road. When I got out to see what I could see, I found that the right front tire was completely flat—just like that!—with a cassie thorn protruding proudly from the tread. This was the early 1980's—no cell phones. With no phone and with back problems besides (which jolting over the washboard roads did nothing to ease), I had only one choice—to wait for some kind soul to come by and help. I was lucky. A car with two young men stopped quite soon and they cheerfully removed the flat tire and mounted the spare for me. I thanked them profusely and went on my way, anxious about disappointing the young library patrons waiting for my program. When I arrived, about thirty-five minutes late, I was greeted by a nice crowd of children, milling around and completely unperturbed by the delay. *Oh, right,* I remembered. *I'm in Antigua, where all schedules are approximate and subject to change. Nobody cares but me.* The program went fine and I learned not to worry so much.

We live in a rural part of Iowa now, on a gravel road. When it rains, gravel and the mud under it become slippery and treacherous. We have ice storms in the winter, which convert pavement into glistening skating rinks. Now and then, deer leap onto the road in front of us without warning, causing our hearts to skip a beat. I'm sure every place has its hazards and they are always unnerving. So it must be the magic of time and distance, but somehow, when I think back on our adventures trying to find our way and avoid obstacles on Antiguan roads, I remember them with more fondness than frustration.

Contrast

The Bahá'í Movement is not an otherworldly, an ascetic, or an esoteric religion. Its teachings are for all, and apply to this life as well as to the next. Its aim is to make this life happy, just and perfect—to establish on earth the Kingdom of heaven. It does not say to the poor man, 'Submit to your poverty and degradation, for greater will be your glory in heaven.' It says: 'Poverty is a social crime. It must not exist. Every man has the right to secure work and by it the sufficient means to meet his daily needs. There cannot continue to exist the vast extremes of wealth and poverty.' To the capitalist… it says: 'Share your profits with your workmen.

(Stanwood Cobb, *Star of the West* Volume X:8, August 1, 1919)

We made friends who worked at one of the posh resorts on the Island and, as a result, had a standing invitation for Sunday morning beach volleyball. We went quite often. But we always felt a slight twinge of guilt as we turned off the bumpy, run-down road and entered the carefully-maintained driveway, lined with precisely-spaced palm trees and manicured lawn, that welcomed the mostly foreign guests.

The source of our discomfort was simple—it was the stark contrast between the real, everyday conditions of life for most Antiguans and the showy lavishness of the resort. Many of our village neighbors worked at establishments like this. We saw them walking the mile or more to and from the luxury hotels closest to Willikies daily. But few of them could have afforded to check in as guests. For that matter, WE couldn't have afforded that either, but that didn't ease our discomfort.

Memories of Antigua

It wasn't that locals were unwelcome on the premises. All beaches are public property in Antigua and we often saw villagers of all ages romping or resting on them. It's more that the Antiguans who worked as housekeepers, laundry or maintenance staff, or food or beverage servers seemed to become invisible to the wealthy tourists (mostly Americans or Europeans, some West Indians) who vacationed there. We had many chances to watch interactions between guests and resort staff and, while we rarely saw actual rudeness, there was a consistent attitude of entitled dismissiveness in the treatment of service staff which weighed heavily on us, on behalf of our neighbors and friends. I guess it's the same everywhere—too many materially privileged people take for granted their own importance and, by contrast, the relative insignificance of those around them who are not so privileged, all with no real malicious intent. It's the essence of condescension.

One day I decided to broach the subject with a young woman named Evelyn, who lived down the road from us. She'd taken a shine to Naren and stopped by now and then to visit. She worked as a housekeeper at the resort on Long Bay. I wanted to proceed carefully, lest my assumptions prove to be either offensive or simply wrong, so I started by asking how she liked her job. It was fine, she said. She was lucky to have a job so close to home, as she also took care of her aging mother.

"Is it very hard work?" I asked.

"I'm strong," she answered. "I don't mind."

"I'll bet you're tired when you come home."

"Yes, Ma'am!"

"Do you have friends at work?"

"Some of us talk and have fun together."

"Do you see them outside of work?"

"Not often. Too tired and too busy."

"Do you ever make friends with the guests?"

"Oh, no, we're supposed to leave them alone and not bother them. We clean when they're out."

"So what happens if you're cleaning and they come back to their room? Do you chat with them?"

"Sometimes. Usually we just leave and come back later. Some of them are nice, but they're on vacation. They don't want to talk to us."

I got a bit braver.

"Does that bother you?"

Evelyn shrugged and glanced away quickly before answering. "Not really. They're the reason I have a job."

She headed home. She didn't exactly confirm my assumptions, but she certainly didn't dispel them.

After that, I kept my eyes and ears open, both on Sunday mornings at the resort and around my neighbors. I heard bits of conversations, not meant to include me, that confirmed a sort of love/hate relationship between many Antiguans and the tourists whose money largely fueled their economy.

Don't get me wrong—Antiguans weren't helpless victims in these transactions. Actually, it was common practice for street vendors to charge tourists significantly more than residents for their wares, and some stores were noticeably pricier during high tourist season. (We threatened to have T-shirts made proclaiming, "We're not tourists, we live here!") But those tourists visited briefly and often experienced little but the delicious relaxation and pampering they expected. It's what drew them to the Island in the first place. Few had meaningful conversations or made friends with actual Antiguans. They left their dollars behind, but nothing of themselves.

I wondered if tourists even noticed, as they made their way from the harbor or the airport to their beach hotels, the villages they passed through. Village houses might sport cheerfully colorful exteriors, but they were generally small. Many were balanced atop cement blocks to stay dry during the rainy season and were often cobbled together from odd panels of corrugated metal or constructed over years from concrete blocks, literally block by block as finances allowed. Did the wealthy vacationers even see the stark contrast between the relative poverty and ramshackle appearance of the villages and the glittering elegance of their luxury accommodations?

We have since been able, on occasion, to travel in relative luxury and to visit gorgeous tropical destinations with other well-to-do travelers, and we've enjoyed it all. But I always try to take a minute to notice the name tags or listen to the introductions of those who serve us along the way, and to remember and call them by their names. I try to picture them with families, as parents or siblings, sons or daughters, to really see them and appreciate their efforts, and perhaps leave a good tip. Because they could be, and for a while were, my neighbors, with dreams and needs and hopes much like mine, and they are sharing their home with me.

"Squeeze the Eyes!"

Eat ye, O people, of the good things which God hath allowed you, and deprive not yourselves from His wondrous bounties. Render thanks and praise unto him, and be of them that are truly thankful. (Bahá'u'lláh, *Gleanings from the Writings of Bahá'u'lláh*, 1983 edition, p. 276)

July of 1983 was rainy and stormy, as expected during hurricane season. We didn't experience a hurricane during our time in Antigua, but certainly saw our share of thunderstorms, featuring torrential cloudbursts. By this time, the children were well-integrated into village life and had many friends.

One evening a group of boys collected outside our house, calling for "Natwain." We were finishing dinner, so Nathan hopped up and ran to join them. He rushed in a few minutes later, breathless and eager.

"I need a sack! And a flashlight! We're going crabbing!"

We had no idea what he was talking about. As we questioned him, we realized that he had little idea what he was talking about, either, except that it was very exciting and the guys wanted him to go. While he searched through the carport for something resembling a burlap sack, we went out to see what all the fuss was about.

"What are you guys up to?" we asked Bertsfield and Deberne. "What's this about 'crabbing?'"

"The crabs are running! We're going to catch them!"

When we convinced them that we didn't understand and needed more information, they slowed down enough for a sketchy description of their plans. The local land crabs, which rarely made an appearance, loved the stormy, rainy weather and chose evenings like this to swarm across fields and roadways. This was vital information because, it seemed, said crabs were very, very delicious when cooked. The boys could hardly stand still, so restless were they to head out into the darkening evening with their sacks and a variety of flashlights and homemade torches, to stock up on the delicacies. We pointed out that Nathan had never hunted crabs before. Was it safe? What did we need to know?

Nothing to it, they insisted. They'd walk around the village, looking for swarms. When they found one, each boy would catch as many as he could stuff in his sack, to cook and enjoy for the next week or so.

"How do you catch them?"

"You just grab them, see? And put them in your sack."

"How big are they? Do they have claws? How do you grab them?"

Their impatience grew as we interrogated them and Nathan gathered the necessary tools of the crab-catching trade. They fidgeted in their eagerness to be off, Deberne's torch dancing and sputtering in the drizzle. We didn't want them to be sorry they'd invited Nathan along, so we provided a couple of extra flashlights and sent them on their way, still somewhat wary. We sat on the covered gallery to see what we could see as the evening wore on. Our down-the-road neighbor, Lucette, waved as she walked home from work and accepted our invitation to watch with us.

What we saw was remarkable—small roving gangs of boys, weirdly shadowed in the light of flashlights and smoking torches, walking briskly and quietly until they found a swarm. Then there was a lengthy, chaotic flurry of activity, after which they moved on.

But the most entertaining part was what we heard! We quickly figured out that the crabs did, indeed, have claws, and strong ones. The boys would charge into floods of swarming crabs, grabbing for their shells and emitting wild yelps and frantic shouts of "Squeeze the eyes! Squeeze the eyes!" as the crabs did their best to defend themselves, clamping onto the fingers and toes of their would-be captors. Lucette explained that, when a crab pinched your hand or foot in its claws, the only way to get it to release was to firmly pinch its eye sockets. At first, we assumed that the shouts were the boys with experience, instructing the inexperienced hunters. But as we watched closer encounters, we realized that even the older boys, for all their bravado, had little tolerance for pain and were actually screaming for their fellows to rescue them!

After our initial alarm and Lucette's reassurance that the boys would be fine, we found ourselves laughing until we cried over the slapstick comedy routine playing out over and over around us, characterized by random scrambling, hilariously frantic waving of hands or feet with fist-sized crabs flapping off the ends, accompanied by much shouting about "squeezing the eyes," and followed quickly by victory whoops and leaps as the burlap sacks filled with squirming, writhing crabs protesting their fate. Much later, Nathan returned home carrying a half-full sack, strutting with the pride of a mighty hunter and flaunting several mildly painful battle wounds.

The crabs, once caught, had to be boiled in large pots of water to yield up their meaty sweetness. The boys realized that we were often home mid-afternoon, when they were getting out of school and longing for a snack. They'd come home with Nathan, hoping we would put water on to boil for them, as our kitchen stove made this job much faster and easier than their coal pots. We were happy to oblige and settled into a routine of filling our largest cooking pot with water about half an hour before school got out, so it would be bubbling and ready.

The boys took to hanging their carefully marked burlap sacks (lest anyone try to claim a crab that wasn't his) in our carport. They'd walk Nathan home, grab a crab or two, toss them in the pot, and then squat on the stoop or gallery to dig out and savor every last morsel from the crusty crustacean bodies. It was a cheerful ritual which allowed us to visit and get to know the boys better. If they were feeling generous, they'd share the bounty with us and even with girls in the neighborhood, proving themselves worthy providers and giving us good reason to "be truly thankful" for "the good things which God allowed us."

We were happy spectators through several evenings of crab-hunting mayhem during the season. We enjoyed the raucous entertainment and the delicious treats. And for many years to come, if things got gloomy or stressful and we needed to lighten the mood, one of us would hop around shouting "Squeeze the eyes! Squeeze the eyes!" and we'd dissolve into helpless laughter.

It Seemed Like a Good Idea at the Time…

Keep them ever in safety beneath Thine all-protecting eye. Assist them to exalt Thy Word; make Thou their hearts to be constant in Thy love; strengthen Thou their backs that they may serve Thee well; in servitude, strengthen Thou their powers. ('Abdu'l-Bahá: Quoted in *Advent of Divine Justice*, 1938, p.32)

Looking back, I am startled, even shocked, by how quickly we adapted our thinking to our new cultural context. I'm sure adaptability is a good thing, but I shudder at some of the things we accepted and took in stride because they were so commonplace and natural on the Island. I've already described piling too many kids into our little car (forget even the idea of seat belts) for the ride to the beach and Nathan shinnying up coconut trees to retrieve the fruit for us. Here are more examples.

Dan, a nice young man down the road, befriended our kids. They spent some time together, in the age-fluid way that Antiguan village socializing seemed to work. Dan had a couple of horses, which Nathan and Naren enjoyed visiting and tending. One evening Bob and I were washing dishes under a window that faced the road. Suddenly, we heard a racket of whoops and clattering and looked up just in time to see Dan race by at breakneck speed on one of the horses, with Nathan right behind him on the other—bareback and clinging for dear life! I'm sure I turned white; I know I dropped the dish I was washing. We ran outside but they were long gone. When, to our enormous relief, Nathan returned a while later all in one piece, he simply didn't understand what all the fuss was about! He'd had the time of his life, terrified or not.

A frightening postscript to that event was the evening, a few months later, when a neighbor shouted frantically from the road, begging us to drive Dan to the hospital after he was kicked by one of his usually docile horses. We did, of course, and Dan eventually recovered from the resulting head injury. We never learned what upset the horse, but our kids didn't need us to advise them to keep their distance from then on.

Every man and boy in the village seemed to carry around a machete, a sort of broad-bladed axe, as an all-purpose tool. We didn't own one and, of course, didn't give Nathan one. But we also didn't flinch when the boys he was playing with had them and used them around him. They handled them with skill and we never saw them used aggressively, even in play. One afternoon Nathan and some boys brought several coconuts they had harvested from trees near the beach into our carport. We ran outside (again) when we heard the howl and found Nathan in a near-faint, having cut open his big toe! It turns out that using your foot to stabilize a coconut while you swing at it with a machete is not a good plan. A trip to the emergency room in St. John's, where our friend Seema, an ER nurse, managed to stitch him up, and a few days of healing time, and he was good as new, and definitely wiser! He still carries the scar.

On one of our trips around the Island with our Bahá'í teaching team, we were walking along the historic shoreline of Nelson's Dockyard, where Admiral Horatio Nelson lived and commanded British Naval activity some 200 years earlier. The area is a tourist attraction and is quaint and charming to the eye, but less so to the nose. The water is infamously polluted, or was at the time. Naren saw several children hopping and running along the narrow stone wall that supported the walkway leading to the marina below. Of course, she had to follow suit. We called her back twice, warning her about the dangers of falling into the murky water. But she was six! Of course, she didn't listen and we were busy discussing our tasks for the day. We heard the yelp and the splash almost simultaneously.

Bob sprang into action and managed to fish her out almost immediately, hauling her up by the waistband of her shorts. He dropped her on the grass where she lay, soggy, wretched, and retching. We raced her to a nearby business, hosed her off as best we could, and headed home to get her into a shower and clean clothes. We envisioned all manner of ill effects, from pustulating skin rashes to vomitus stomach distress. We were honestly relieved when we checked on her in bed that night and her skin was not giving off a radioactive glow! She was, apparently, no worse for the experience, aside from a little trauma, and gained some of that common sense that only comes from sobering life experience.

A few months after our arrival, we decided to plant a little garden in a corner of our yard. We sent the kids out to remove some rocks from the chosen site. A few minutes later, Naren ran in wide-eyed and said we'd better "come right now!" We followed her out and found Nathan, standing frozen in place with an expression of pure panic on his face. We followed his gaze to the papaya-sized rock in his hand and then to the depression in the ground where it had been, which was occupied by a fist-sized, brown, and hairy tarantula! We knew there were tarantulas on the Island but had, as yet, not met one in person, and this was a genuinely impressive specimen.

Again, Bob came to the rescue. He grabbed Nathan and we retreated into the house. If only we'd known then what we soon learned—that tarantulas are slow, lazy creatures. You practically have to beg them to "attack." Even if they do bite, their venom is unlikely to cause more than a few days of pain and mild sickness, and then only if you are sensitive to it. On the upside, they consume large quantities of insects and so, almost like the little lizards that we'd learned to welcome into our home (and encourage to bring their friends), they can be a blessing. A friend of ours in Parham had one that seemed to live in his shower. He reacted philosophically, naming it and talking to it while he bathed! But at age eight, and as ignorant as we all were about such matters, Nathan's short life must have flashed before his eyes in that brief moment.

We were guilty of a similar blunder when, still suffering from middle-class Americans' aversion to bugs of various kinds in the house, we got the bright idea to spray insecticide around the outside perimeter. Remember the "so pretty" centipede we encountered early in our stay? Well, it turns out that it had a whole clan of siblings, aunts, uncles, and cousins who lived peacefully, minding their own business, in the ground and under the brush along the base of the house, along with a host of other more and less desirable small critters. When we disrupted their ecosystem they, understandably, fled into the open, effectively grounding us inside for a couple of days until they died or dispersed, or the poison wore off and they settled back in. From then on, we left them alone to live out of sight, peacefully minding their own business.

Before we left Utah to move to Antigua, my parents expressed concern about our physical wellbeing in home. We were doing meaningful work that seemed to be bearing good fruit. We still held out some hope. Naren and I would fly to Iowa to stay with friends and get a proper diagnosis for a minor but persistent health problem she was having while Bob pursued one last possible job opportunity. Depending on the outcome of both things, either Naren and I would return to Antigua or Bob and Nathan would join us in Iowa to regroup and make a fresh start. Either way, it was time to act. We booked our flight.

A few days before Naren's and my departure we were puttering around in the house, getting ready. We heard, through the open windows, the polite call, "Inside! Inside!" We went to the door and were very surprised to find, standing on the road, two elderly women whom we immediately recognized but hadn't gotten to know well. They were prominent in the village, matriarchs of a sort. Though of different height and build, they both stood tall and carried themselves with great dignity. We couldn't imagine what had prompted this unexpected visit, but invited them in with as warm a welcome as we could muster. They settled with Bob in the living room while I made and served tea. We sat and sipped. We made a couple of awkward attempts at conversation, which never got past polite, one-word responses. Then nothing. In typical Antiguan style, they said not a word. The next several minutes felt like hours to us—as Americans, we had never managed to acquire the Antiguans' ease with silence. If they sensed our tension and were amused by it, they didn't let on. Their faces were expressionless.

Finally, when our discomfort was becoming acute, the taller woman spoke.

"We heard you were leaving."

We confirmed, with a brief, fumbling attempt at explanation and regret, that we might have to make that choice.

"We don't want you to leave," she said. "We've gotten used to you."

Now that may not sound like high praise to you. But it was music to our ears! These honored, regal women, with whom we'd had little direct contact, had come to accept us and welcome our presence. It felt huge to us—both a validation and an added weight on our regret.

As I recall, our guests stood up, shortly after that pronouncement, and took their leave. They had said what they came to say; they had accomplished their task. For our part, we were touched beyond measure. They'd gotten used to us!

Reflecting

O Lord! Grant Thine infinite bestowals, and let the light of Thy guidance shine. Illumine the eyes, gladden the hearts with abiding joy. Confer a new spirit upon all people and bestow upon them eternal life. Unlock the gates of true understanding and let the light of faith shine resplendent. Gather all people beneath the shadow of Thy bounty and cause them to unite in harmony, so that they may become as the rays of one sun, as the waves of one ocean, and as the fruit of one tree. May they drink from the same fountain. May they be refreshed by the same breeze. May they receive illumination from the same source of light. Thou art the Giver, the Merciful, the Omnipotent. ('Abdu'l-Bahá, *Bahá'í Prayers*, 1991 edition, p. 101)

We didn't get to stay in Antigua as long as we'd hoped. Circumstances beyond our control sent us back to the States after only sixteen months. But that period is one of the richest in my life and left a strong imprint on our family. We were able to serve, in small, humble ways, and to feel we had made some difference to the Bahá'í community and to the people around us. We formed lifelong friendships. We learned important, quiet lessons that helped our spirits and characters grow. We experienced what it means to be in the minority in society, in several ways. We came to a profound new understanding of materialism, and of what it means and what it takes to be happy. We felt genuine kinship with people who were, to outward seeming, quite different from us.

To this day, when I find myself caught up in America's frantic pace, when everyday stresses threaten to overwhelm me and I need to relax deeply, I send my mind back to glorious, prayerful sunrises on Shirley Heights or to lazy, sun-warmed, ocean breeze-cooled afternoons at Rendezvous Bay, and stresses melt away.

I am grateful beyond measure for this unique episode in my life and the life of my family, for the people who patiently helped us through it, and for the deep sense of Divine guidance and protection that surrounded us.

> "God-amighty nebber shut him eyes.
> Fu true, fu true."

ABOUT THE AUTHOR

Diane Findlay is an avid reader with
a Master's Degree in Library Science from the
University of Iowa. She has worked as a
public librarian, administrator for an
international student exchange organization,
and freelance writer. She is the author of several
teacher resource books as well as BEMUSED,
a middle grades fiction book.

A country girl at heart, Diane lives in rural Iowa,
where she stays active with family, friends,
and the Bahá'í community, and from which
she and her husband travel the world.

**For more information about the Bahá'í Faith,
visit www.bahai.org.**

www.ingramcontent.com/pod-product-compliance
Lightning Source LLC
Chambersburg PA
CBHW061337040426
42444CB00011B/2966